Author's Email: bob@smsrd.com

Book an Appointment calendly.com/mission-is-sales-book/30min

Smoking Hot Marketing Ideas

Sparks to Ignite a Marketing Brainstorm

SMS knows marketing, and we have put some of the best ideas we've learned into the pages that follow. Pick the ones you like and light a fire under your marketing.

Library of Congress Cataloging-in-Publication Data

Dumouchel, Robert, author.

2021 Smoking Hot Digital Marketing Ideas

Library of Congress Control Number: 2021907338

ISBN 978-0-9982139-5-8

Table of Contents

How to use this Book

This Book is designed to help your business run a productive marketing plan brainstorming meeting. This Book seeds the idea phase and gets your team's creative juices running. The best ideas will come from your team, and this book is the competition they need to beat. So, let the games begin!

Pitch

Each page in the body of the Book is an idea followed by the pitch. If, after reading the pitch, the idea lacks gravity, then move on. At the pitch level, your rejection rate should be 90% or more. Most annual plans will have the continuing support of things that work and 3-4 new ideas to drive the **"What's Next?"** plan. The pitch is written in the voice of someone attending the meeting.

Clarification

DO NOT read the clarification paragraph if the pitch did not excite the team. Anything past the first paragraph is just building on the basic concept. If the first paragraph did not sell the idea, then the rest is a waste of your time.

Minimum Test Period

We include a minimum recommended test period on each idea page, but these are only guesstimates, and they require your due diligence during the next planning step.

Codes

The last lines on the idea page are the codes. These encode the channel, cost, industries, and locations. You will find these in the index at the end of the Book. If you are looking for all the PPC ideas, there is a list in the index.

Channels

Code	Description
PPC-S	Pay Per Click - Search
PPC-D	Pay Per Click – Display
SEO	Search Engine Optimization
SM	Social Media
EM	Email
PD	Podcast
PH	Phone
TC	Teleconference – Zoom
All	All channels

All the channel codes are indexed, so if you want to see all the PPC ideas, you will find them in the index at the end of the Book.

Project Coding

Each idea is coded with the profile of the project to communicate the profile of the idea quickly. Factors are cost, time, risk, and return on investment with ranks from zero to three.

- Rank 0 - Zero – no cost or effort
- Rank 1 - Low
- Rank 2 - Medium
- Rank 3 - High

Set-Up Time	1	**Set-Up Cost**	1
Recurring Time	2	**Recurring Cost**	2
Risk	3	**ROI**	3

Each of these codes is indexed at the end of the Book. The index provides a quick way to find all items with a specific ranking. If you want all the low-cost items or high ROI, look it up in the index.

Lots of room to write

Throughout the Book, we leave lots of room to write notes and record new ideas. There are 99 ideas in this Book and room many more from your team. The space reserved for this looks like this.

There are some **"just for fun things"** to keep the creativity up and seed the staff dialog.

Big Goal

When planning marketing ideas, you must first decide on the big goal. Do you want to? (*pick one*):

- **Incrementally** grow your business
- Create **breakaway** growth

For incremental growth, you want solid ideas that have contained risk. For breakaway sales, you are looking for high-risk, high-reward ideas. Less than 20% growth is incremental more than 50% is breakaway.

No specific order

This eBook is a random list of ideas and is not in any priority sequence. Marketing is about painting a picture in your customer's mind, and each idea is one more stroke of the paintbrush.

Our Failure Guarantee

We guarantee that 100% of the ideas you fail to act on will fail 100% of the time. Marketing is legalized gambling, but there are winners and losers. The only guarantee in marketing is that your campaign will fail if you fail to try. This does not mean you should pursue every idea, but you must try something.

Duplications

Within the book, you might notice some ideas that seem to be duplicates of others, which is done on purpose. Some ideas are restated because they were deemed important enough to get a different pitch with different language. Sometimes the same idea from a different perspective using different language will get a different response from your team.

Prepare Your Team

Many years ago, a mentor of mine told me that if you want to double the creativity in a meeting, then hold it out of the office. If you're going to increase the imagination of a team, give them a separate office. If you want to double the creativity again, put the office over the top of a bar.

To get a team ready for a creative session, you need to give them some advance notice and let the meeting's objective ferment for a few days. Encourage risk-taking and say so directly. Leave nothing to the imagination.

Set the Creative Stage

1. Comfortable Seating
2. Comfortable temperature
3. Lots of fresh air
4. Constant feeding and drinks – especially coffee!
5. Take regular breaks – everyone goes for a walk
6. Fun physical objects – especially complex toys that have some assembly required. Think Legos & ROKR
7. Encourage debate and disagreement
8. Include a note-taker, and they should not be part of the creative team
9. Gaming with a gambling element – provide Monopoly Money and bragging right rewards.
10. Visual Show
11. Study focusing music
12. Hold all calls and remove all cell phones and laptops.

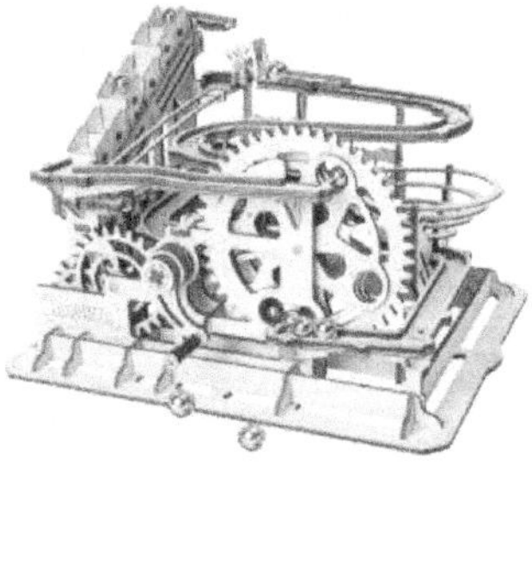

13. Allow only one internet connection for research. Allow only the Note Taker to operate this.
14. Hold the meeting off-premises.
15. Start the meeting with a creative and cooperative activity.
16. Hire a facilitator or appoint one from staff. Try to avoid making it the highest-ranking person in the room.

Meeting Kickoff

The kickoff of a creative meeting is critical. It needs to be high energy and shocking, so it wakes up the creativity. Start with a group activity and have them solve a problem or build something as a group.

Start with a Team activity to get minds moving. We recommend the Marshmallow Challenge. We would love to take credit for this, but alas, it is not ours. The Marshmallow Challenge was developed by Tom Wujec, who has done the activity with hundreds of groups worldwide. Visit the Marshmallow Challenge website for more information.

The Marshmallow Challenge

If you want to know more about this activity's value, this YouTube video provides a management perspective to the activity.
https://www.youtube.com/watch?v=H0_yKBitO8M

Teams of four get the following materials and instructions:

Materials

- 20 sticks of spaghetti
- one yard of masking tape
- one yard of string, include scissors for hard to break string
- A fresh full-sized Marshmallow
- A measuring tape for the judge
- Countdown App or Stopwatch

Instructions:

- Build the Tallest Freestanding Structure: The winning team is the one that has the tallest structure measured from the tabletop surface to the top of the marshmallow.
- The Entire Marshmallow Must be on top.
- Cutting or eating part of the marshmallow disqualifies the team.
- Teams may use as much or as little of the kit as they want
- Teams are free to break the spaghetti, cut up the tape and string.
- The Challenge Lasts 18 minutes.
- Any touching or supporting of the structure disqualifies the team.

1. ABC

Pitch: What if we built an ABC Campaign for our PPC Accounts?

Clarification: ABC represents performance classes of keywords. Sort any PPC account by your primary value, and you will find that just a few keywords will contribute to the majority of the actions you seek. Here is a typical breakdown:

A=Top 5% **B**=Next 10% **C** = Last 85%

If ABC is appropriately run, A will be fully funded and never run out of budget, B will run most of the time, and C will get the leftovers. Keyword rank will need to be recalculated to maintain an ABC campaign properly. ABC is a redistribution of the budget, not a change in the total.

Minimum Test Period: 6 months

Channels: PPC-S

Set-Up Time	2	**Set-Up Cost**	0
Recurring Time	2	**Recurring Cost**	1
Risk	1	**ROI**	2

2. Add a Channel

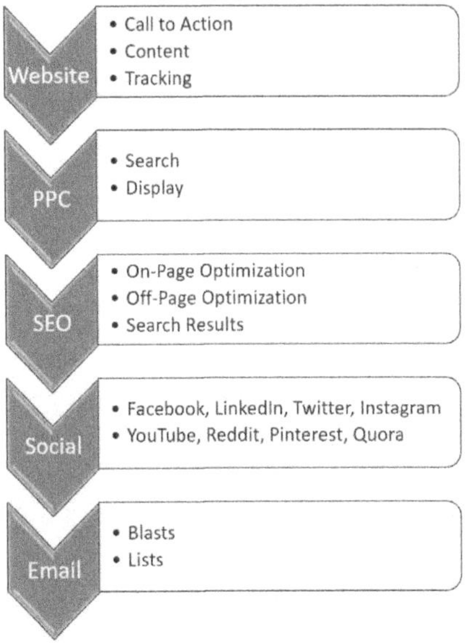

Pitch: What if we added a new channel to our marketing?

Clarification: All businesses must start somewhere, and that leaves some channels not implemented. This idea proposes to add the next logical channel for the business. The graphic here is a standard order of digital channels, but it is not the only strategy. Consideration must be given to dependencies and synergies between the channels. For example, implementing SEO before PPC is a common mistake. SEO takes a long time to start, and PPC data is a tremendous advantage to implementing SEO.

Minimum Test Period: 4 months

Channels: All

Set-Up Time	2	**Set-Up Cost**	1
Recurring Time	1	**Recurring Cost**	2
Risk	2	**ROI**	3

3. Advance a Status

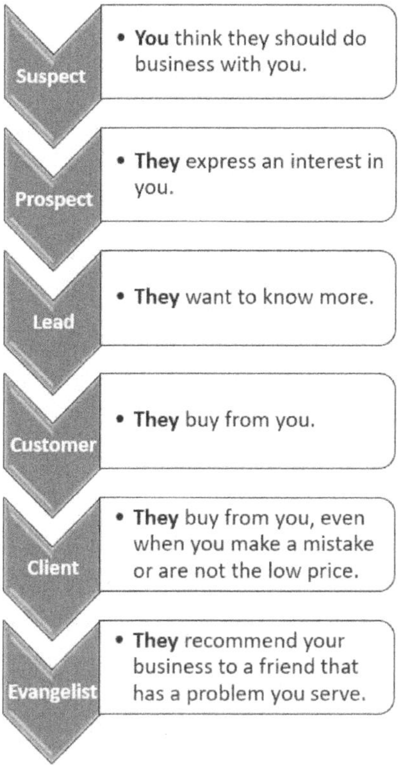

Pitch: What if we develop a campaign to advance a status within a channel?

Clarification: Many campaigns have unrealistic goals in a single contact, and this is about creating focus. Reducing your ask in a campaign increases the conversion percentage but reduces the value of the conversion. A typical example is targeting a sales lead versus an email subscription. The Email advances from suspect to prospect, but the lead progresses from suspect to lead. The problem is that you will get fewer leads than free subscriptions. Ask would you rather have ten emails or a sales lead?

Minimum Test Period: 4 months

Channels: All

Set-Up Time	2	**Set-Up Cost**	1
Recurring Time	1	**Recurring Cost**	1
Risk	2	**ROI**	2

4. Advance a Stage

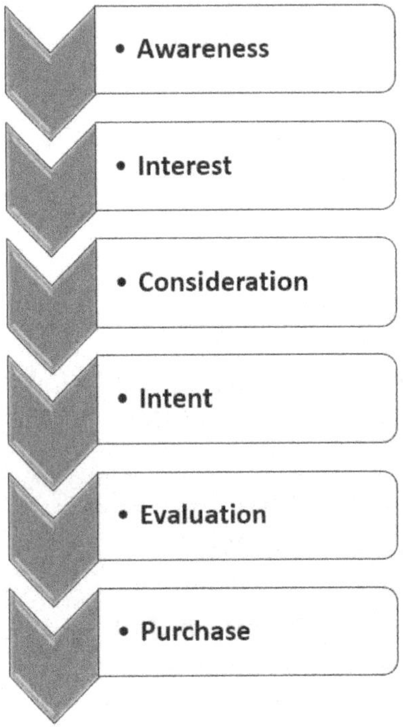

Pitch: What if we created a campaign to advance one of the stages within a lead?

Clarification: If you cannot measure it, you cannot improve it. Find a way to measure movement from one stage to another and then develop a campaign to advance the stage.

Minimum Test Period: 4 months

Channels: All

Set-Up Time	2	**Set-Up Cost**	1
Recurring Time	1	**Recurring Cost**	1
Risk	2	**ROI**	2

5. Airplanes

Pitch: What if we jumped out of a perfectly good airplane with a business banner and landed at a big event?

Clarification: This is about creating an event worth talking about. The airplane could be something entirely different as long as it is **outrageous**. Find the most significant event in your area and find out how far outside the rules this is. Stop one step short of getting arrested but create something people talk about for years.

Minimum Test Period: 3 Months

Channels: PPC-D, SEO, SM

Set-Up Time	3	**Set-Up Cost**	1
Recurring Time	1	**Recurring Cost**	3
Risk	3	**ROI**	3

6. Appreciation Gifts

Pitch: What if we sent appreciation gifts to customers at personally meaningful times for them?

Clarification: Building relationships is a complicated process, and sometimes that it is necessary to say thank you. Appreciation gifts can serve this, but they have to be authentic. This is not a one size fits all idea. For some, this is done during holiday seasons, but the best is when it is personal.

Minimum Test Period: 12 Months

Channels: SM

Set-Up Time	3	**Set-Up Cost**	1
Recurring Time	1	**Recurring Cost**	2
Risk	2	**ROI**	3

7. Authority

Pitch: What if we created a campaign based on building authority?

Clarification: Create a campaign designed to promote the business as an authority in the industry. Write a book, conduct a seminar, get interviewed by the media, and other things. Many of the other ideas in this book contribute to your authority.

Minimum Test Period: 4 Months

Channels: PPC-D, SM

Set-Up Time	2	**Set-Up Cost**	1
Recurring Time	1	**Recurring Cost**	2
Risk	3	**ROI**	1

8. Backlinks

Pitch: What if we build a campaign to build backlinks to our website and blog articles?

Clarification: Earned backlinks are the most challenging task in SEO, and the quality of the backlink, meaning its source, is the most critical factor in the backlink. One hundred links from no-name sites are worth zero, but one link for a big name is pure SEO gold. Be very careful with any partners that help you with this campaign. There are many true stories of SEO firms that have destroyed a website's reputation with poor-quality backlinks.

Minimum Test Period: 12-24 months

Channels: SEO

Set-Up Time	1	**Set-Up Cost**	1
Recurring Time	3	**Recurring Cost**	3
Risk	3	**ROI**	3

9. Become One

Pitch: What if we create a campaign to increase our empathy toward our customer's challenges?

Clarification: Your inner Yoda says, "***Become one with your Customers.***" Understand what causes customer's pain and pleasure and genuinely empathize with them. Learn to **truly feel their pain**! Create a campaign focused on that, feel that, be that.

To understand the customer's pain, you must get down to a specific segment of your customers. Whom are we talking about? How do we reach them? How do we soothe their pain?

Minimum Test Period: 4 Months

Channels: All

Set-Up Time	3	**Set-Up Cost**	1
Recurring Time	3	**Recurring Cost**	3
Risk	3	**ROI**	3

10. Birds of a Feather

Pitch: What if we created a remarketing campaign to find sites that customers frequent? Then use those sites in a Placement Targeted Display Campaign.

Clarification: The concept of **"Birds of a Feather"** is that they flock together. Follow where your customers go with a broadly targeted remarketing campaign, and you will know where your best prospects are. Using the websites from the remarketing as placement targeting, you can zero in on prospects' most likely-to-visit sites.

Minimum Test Period: 4 months

Channels: PPC-D, SM

Set-Up Time	3	**Set-Up Cost**	1
Recurring Time	3	**Recurring Cost**	3
Risk	3	**ROI**	3

11. Blog Optimization

Pitch: What if we took all our blog articles in popularity order and optimized them for their target keywords?

Clarification: Blog articles degrade over time, and publication standards are changed. This project would clean up and remove the sins of the past and examine the on-page optimization. We can clean out old articles that no longer contribute to our traffic and put 301 redirects or canonical URLs to the home or blog page.

Minimum Test Period: 3 months

Channels: SEO

Set-Up Time	3	**Set-Up Cost**	1
Recurring Time	3	**Recurring Cost**	3
Risk	3	**ROI**	3

12. Book Recommendations

Pitch: What if we had every person with good customer relationships asked for a book recommendation?

Clarification: This includes all customer-facing employees, Sales Reps, CEO, CMO, Customer Service, and others. Read the recommended Book, have a conversation with the customer, and write a summary. Put the Book and summary in the company library and do a "Book Report" at the next staff meeting. Post the summary on our social media, with the customer name, if authorized.

Minimum Test Period: 12 months or more

Channels: SM

Set-Up Time	1	**Set-Up Cost**	1
Recurring Time	2	**Recurring Cost**	1
Risk	1	**ROI**	3

13. Bounce Rate

Pitch: What if we could improve our bounce rate by 10% in search, display, or organic?

Clarification: Bounce is one of many measurements, and most bounce problems can be traced to content challenges. The "Measure and it shall improve" effect is what we are after here. Many factors can influence bounce rates, but most are simply a mismatch between the visitor's wants and what we think is their need. Talking about price when the pain point is quality is an example of this mismatch.

Minimum Budget: Low execution, High research

Minimum Test Period: 12 months or more

Channels: PPC-S, PPC-D

Set-Up Time	1	**Set-Up Cost**	1
Recurring Time	1	**Recurring Cost**	1
Risk	2	**ROI**	3

14. Business Awards

Pitch: What if we inventory all the potential awards in our industry, community, and other areas and then go after those. We create an annual calendar for the start and end of the submission periods and compete in all the possible awards. Media outlets are constantly looking for great local stories, so let us be one.

Clarification: This is an organization and execution campaign that we cannot win if we do not show up. 50% of the competition is simply showing up.

Minimum Test Period: 1 time

Channels: PR

Set-Up Time	2	**Set-Up Cost**	1
Recurring Time	3	**Recurring Cost**	2
Risk	1	**ROI**	2

15. Business Audiences

Pitch: What if we created a campaign focused on the significant B2B audience types?

Group	Motivated by
Technicians	Quality of the Work
Managers	Dependability
Sales	Personal Relationship
Entrepreneurs	What's Next?

Clarification: Many campaigns fail to target specific audience profiles. By using a specific target, we can put issues vital to them in the materials. This focuses marketing content on topics that are important to the audience.

Minimum Test Period: 1 time

Channels: All

Set-Up Time	**1**	**Set-Up Cost**	**1**
Recurring Time	**1**	**Recurring Cost**	**1**
Risk	**1**	**ROI**	**2**

16. Budget Balancing

Pitch: What if we calculated the maximum budget for all campaigns based on their impression share then distributed the budget equally based on that?

Clarification: This is budget redistribution based on the priority across the ecosystem pipeline. The concept is to give a smoother flow from the budget to the priority in the sales pipeline.

Channel

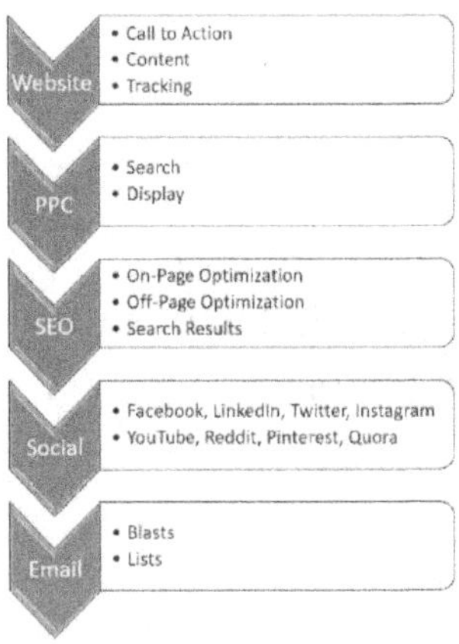

Status

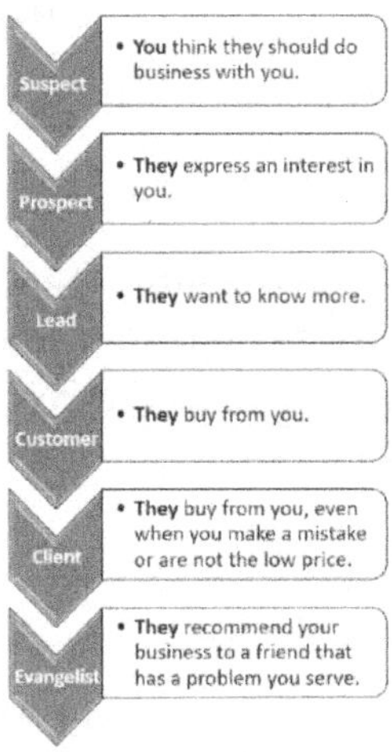

Stage

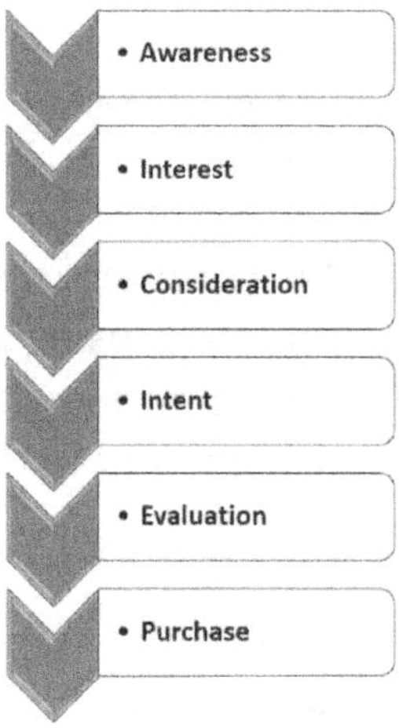

Minimum Test Period: 4 months

Channels: PPC-S, PPC-D

Cost:

Set-Up Time	2	**Set-Up Cost**	0
Recurring Time	1	**Recurring Cost**	0
Risk	2	**ROI**	2

17. Budget Experiments

Pitch: What if we created a budget for high-risk, high reward campaigns?

Clarification: Return on Investment must be 10x or better, and the expected success rate should be no more than 25%. The campaign goal is to get employees to take enough risk.

Minimum Budget: 10% of total marketing budget

Minimum Test Period: 4 months

Channels: PPC-S, PPC-D

Set-Up Time	1	**Set-Up Cost**	1
Recurring Time	2	**Recurring Cost**	2
Risk	3	**ROI**	2

18. Breakout Idea

Pitch: What if we could find an idea that would create more than 100% growth?

Clarification: Breakout ideas hold the potential of growing our business by more than 100% in the next year. On this topic, talk only about BIG IDEAS, nothing incremental. Would it be a new product, new industry, a new offer, or new business?

Minimum Budget: TBE

Minimum Test Period: 6 months

Channels: All

Set-Up Time	3	**Set-Up Cost**	1
Recurring Time	2	**Recurring Cost**	1
Risk	3	**ROI**	3

19. Bring-em Back

Pitch: What if we could bring back lost customers?

Clarification: What would a campaign to bring back lost customers look like? Inventory all lost accounts for the last several years. Classify, sort, and tally all lost customers and the known or likely reasons for the loss. With this data, can we make those reasons go away by removing barriers and reopening communications? Rebuilding trust is difficult but not impossible.

Minimum Test Period: 6 months

Channels: EM

Set-Up Time	**1**	**Set-Up Cost**	**1**
Recurring Time	**3**	**Recurring Cost**	**1**
Risk	**1**	**ROI**	**3**

20. B2B, B2C, D2C

Pitch: What if we could open another market for our business?

Clarification: Are we missing any significant markets?

- Business to Business (B2B)
- Business to Consumer (B2C)
- Direct to Consumer (D2C)

Can our products or services be sold into a non-traditional market? Do we have synergies or cost savings that can be leveraged? This idea could require repackaging or rethinking our market messaging.

Minimum Test Period: 6 months

Channels: SM, PPC-Display, EM

Set-Up Time	3	**Set-Up Cost**	2
Recurring Time	2	**Recurring Cost**	2
Risk	2	**ROI**	3

21. Catch a Customer

Pitch: What if we could catch a customer doing something great?

Clarification: Using all the volume of our social media and advertising, tell the world how great they are? This must be authentic, or the world will see through this in a millisecond. We have had many discussions on how to increase referrals in our marketing. The best way to get others to talk about us is to talk about them. The Reciprocity Rule starts this by listening carefully to events involving our customers and prospects.

Minimum Test Period: 4 months

Channels: SM, PPC-D

Set-Up Time	1	**Set-Up Cost**	1
Recurring Time	2	**Recurring Cost**	2
Risk	1	**ROI**	3

22. Catch an Employee

Pitch: What if we could catch an employee doing something great?

Clarification: This is a variant of the Catch a Customer campaign. Give the employee an innovative non-monetary reward and tell the world at the top of your voice. This one can be seen as self-serving, so we have to be careful not to overdo this.

Minimum Test Period: 12 months

Channels: SM, PPC-D, EM

Set-Up Time	**1**	**Set-Up Cost**	**1**
Recurring Time	**1**	**Recurring Cost**	**1**
Risk	**1**	**ROI**	**2**

23. Commission a Mural

Pitch: What if we commissioned a Mural on a building and connected it to our brand?

Clarification: Many cities are open to the creation of building art, especially on ugly buildings. You must get the owner and city planning to agree to this, but the impact can be huge. Cities large and small have building art programs, including Los Angeles, San Francisco, New York City, Honolulu, Miami, and tiny Eureka, California. It would help if you found a synergy between the art and your brand, but it is worth the effort. Even better than a city art project would be to do this to our building.

Minimum Budget: $10k+

Minimum Test Period: 3 years

Channels: SM, PPC-D, EM

Set-Up Time	3	**Set-Up Cost**	3
Recurring Time	0	**Recurring Cost**	1
Risk	1	**ROI**	3

24. Call Tracking

Pitch: What if we installed call tracking on all sales phone lines and audited them for opportunities to improve sales training?

Clarification: Inbound sales phone lines are gold mines in every business, but sometimes they bleed gold. The simple act of tracking and training will improve results by at least 20%.

Minimum Test Period: 6 months

Channels: PH

Set-Up Time	2	**Set-Up Cost**	1
Recurring Time	3	**Recurring Cost**	1
Risk	1	**ROI**	2

25. Caption Contest

Pitch: What if we held a caption contest for our ads?

Clarification: Engaging our audience with a contest gets them to buy into the content, and people love contests. Contests can build your fan base in social media and serve as a rich source of marketing data. Use voting in your contest to raise the engagement level.

Minimum Test Period: 3 months

Channels: SM

Set-Up Time	2	**Set-Up Cost**	1
Recurring Time	2	**Recurring Cost**	2
Risk	2	**ROI**	3

26. Conventions

Pitch: What if we attended an industry or customer convention?

Clarification: Conventions and Conferences represent a focused marketing opportunity. Roles in this can be as an attendee, exhibitor, or speaker. As an attendee, we need a plan that connects to the customers. Ideally, the first time should be as an attendee to get the lay of the land, then upgrade to an exhibitor, and ultimately as a subject expert speaker.

Minimum Test Period: 2 Years

Channels: SM

Set-Up Time	**1**	**Set-Up Cost**	**2**
Recurring Time	**2**	**Recurring Cost**	**2**
Risk	**2**	**ROI**	**2**

27. Community Connector

Pitch: What if we helped customers connect to others that might be important to them?

Clarification: Have everyone look at their contacts and evaluate the value of an introduction between them. People value connections to others and view the facilitators of that highly. An interesting side effect of this practice is a reciprocal connection to someone you want to meet.

Minimum Test Period: 6 months

Channels: SM

Set-Up Time	**1**	**Set-Up Cost**	**1**
Recurring Time	**2**	**Recurring Cost**	**1**
Risk	**2**	**ROI**	**3**

28. Community Builder

Pitch: What if we built a helpful community for our customers?

Clarification: Community builders are held in high regard in social media, and this does not happen by accident. Thriving communities have at their core an evangelist that made it happen through the power of their personality. Being that person separates us, in the eyes of our customers, from our competitors. Community building takes little money but significant time.

Minimum Test Period: 12 months

Channels: SM

Set-Up Time	**3**	**Set-Up Cost**	**1**
Recurring Time	**3**	**Recurring Cost**	**1**
Risk	**1**	**ROI**	**3**

29. Coopetition (Cooperative Competition)

Pitch: What if we find ways to cooperate with our competitors rather than fighting with them?

Clarification: By building partnerships that respect each other's turf, we could create better service for our clients and improved profits for us. Competitors can be great customers. This campaign would work on creating relationships that focus on the partnership and design around the competitive issues.

Minimum Test Period: 4 months

Channels: EM

Set-Up Time	**3**	**Set-Up Cost**	**1**
Recurring Time	**1**	**Recurring Cost**	**1**
Risk	**3**	**ROI**	**2**

30. Certification

Pitch: What if we had one or more of our staff complete a professional certification?

Clarification: Professional certifications are suitable for staff, and they communicate value to our customers. Promoting staff accomplishments is suitable for everyone, and the paid traffic can be very low cost.

Minimum Test Period: 6 months

Channels: SM, PPC-D, SEO, EM

Set-Up Time	3	**Set-Up Cost**	1
Recurring Time	1	**Recurring Cost**	2
Risk	1	**ROI**	3

31. Circle of Influence

Pitch: What if we created a campaign targeting the circle of influence of a strategic prospect?

Clarification: A circle of influence is a campaign that targets the people that report to or have a trust relationship with the decision maker. Many times the final decision maker cannot be directly reached or influenced. They draw their decision from the circle of people around them. In consumers it is best to sell the wife even if the husband seems like the customer. For a CEO the decision will be votes from their VPs.

Minimum Test Period: 12 Months

Channels: All

Set-Up Time	2	**Set-Up Cost**	2
Recurring Time	1	**Recurring Cost**	2
Risk	2	**ROI**	3

32. Deals & Incentives

Pitch: What if we created a deal specific to an up-sell product based on prior purchases?

Clarification: As a business, we know that certain product sales should include an up-sell offer, but we are not perfect at this delivery. This is a scheduled clean-up campaign, so the up-sell offer is consistently presented. Each quarter we put together an offer for customers that bought product x but not product y.

Minimum Test Period: 12 Months

Channels: EM

Set-Up Time	1	**Set-Up Cost**	2
Recurring Time	1	**Recurring Cost**	2
Risk	3	**ROI**	1

33. Disaster or Opportunity

Pitch: What if we created a campaign to leverage a recent disaster?

Clarification: Never waste a perfectly-good disaster is an old business expression because what looks like a disaster often turns out to be an opportunity. The 2020 Pandemic is a case in point. Many businesses had to make significant changes, but these ended up benefiting some businesses in the long run.

Minimum Test Period: 4 months

Channels: SM

Set-Up Time	**3**	**Set-Up Cost**	**1**
Recurring Time	**3**	**Recurring Cost**	**3**
Risk	**3**	**ROI**	**3**

34. Earworm

Pitch: What if we created an earworm for the company, product, or service?

Clarification: An earworm is a catchy song, tune, or jingle that continually runs through a person's mind. Creating these are more art than science, but some people can dependably create this effect. Studies show that this happens to 90% of the population once a week. Here, the trick is to create a strong bond between the earworm and your brand, service, or value.

Minimum Test Period: 3 months

Channels: SM

Set-Up Time	2	**Set-Up Cost**	2
Recurring Time	1	**Recurring Cost**	3
Risk	3	**ROI**	3

35. Fishing

Pitch: What if we created a campaign to get the search query data to grow our PPC campaigns?

Clarification: Fishing in PPC is a process of using a campaign to conduct research rather than driving traffic. This can be used to test competitive brand search and keyword growth searches. It is essential to keep budgets under control in this strategy.

Minimum Test Period: 1 month

Channels: PPC-S

Set-Up Time	1	**Set-Up Cost**	0
Recurring Time	2	**Recurring Cost**	1
Risk	3	**ROI**	1

36. Flushing Assumptions

Pitch: What if we flushed out all the things we think we know and retested everything?

Clarification: What we think we know often causes us to make decisions that we should not. We fail to act because of failures in the past. These "Never do that again" events can accumulate to the point that we fail because we fail to act.

Minimum Test Period: 3 months

Channels: All

Set-Up Time	3	**Set-Up Cost**	1
Recurring Time	3	**Recurring Cost**	3
Risk	3	**ROI**	2

37. Emergency

Pitch: What if we isolated emergency qualified keywords?

Clarification: Emergency traffic is often combined with other less qualified keywords and bid on the ad group's average return. This idea would separate emergency traffic from routine traffic with more aggressive bidding.

Minimum Test Period: 3 months

Channels: PPC-S

Set-Up Time	3	**Set-Up Cost**	1
Recurring Time	3	**Recurring Cost**	3
Risk	3	**ROI**	3

38. Early-Stage Traffic

Pitch: What if we targeted early-stage customers in the research phase of the purchase cycle?

Clarification: Everyone wants the late-stage traffic where the closed sale is just one click away. Unfortunately, it is challenging to step into the flow at that point. How can we get into the flow of the deal earlier? Keywords for early-stage queries are cheaper but take more time to close the deal. This idea requires that we redesign our tracking, measuring, and follow-up.

Minimum Test Period: 4 months

Channels: PPC-S, PPC-D

Set-Up Time	2	**Set-Up Cost**	0
Recurring Time	1	**Recurring Cost**	2
Risk	3	**ROI**	2

39. Farmer's Market

Pitch: What if we introduce our product at a Farmer's Market to get real consumer input?

Clarification: In marketing, they say nothing is like seeing the whites of the buyers' eyes to know what a consumer thinks of your product or service. For a small amount of money, we can set up a booth and put our best salespeople in it to introduce our product or service. We do not have to be a farmer to learn if consumers like our broccoli.

Minimum Test Period: 4 months

Channels: PPC-D

Set-Up Time	2	**Set-Up Cost**	0
Recurring Time	1	**Recurring Cost**	2
Risk	3	**ROI**	2

40. Fear of Loss

Pitch: What if we could create a Fear of Loss for our product or service?

Clarification: Fear of Loss is a primary motivational factor, and the only question is how do we induce this into our visitors? Every year the toy industry has a popular blowout toy where supply is limited, and demand is enormous. They have figured out how to create fear of loss over and over. Look at what happened to toilet paper at the beginning of the pandemic or flags after 9/11. How can we create an imbalance between supply and demand?

Minimum Test Period: 4 Months

Channels: SM, PPC-S, PPC-D

Set-Up Time	2	**Set-Up Cost**	0
Recurring Time	1	**Recurring Cost**	3
Risk	3	**ROI**	3

41. Generations

Pitch: What if we separate a generation and focus our messaging on them?

Clarification: Different generations have different life experiences that cause them to respond differently to different messaging. By isolating one generation, we can focus on the messaging. Can we target products or services to pull on the strings of these life experiences? The closer the message is to the audience, the more influential the campaign will be.

Minimum Test Period: 4 months

Channels: PPC-S, PPC-D, SEO

Set-Up Time	1	**Set-Up Cost**	0
Recurring Time	1	**Recurring Cost**	2
Risk	1	**ROI**	2

42. Google Alerts

Pitch: What if we created alerts for all customers and their competitors and built a follow-up system for opportunities?

Clarification: Timing is the most critical element in marketing, and events drive timing. Well-engineered alerts could inform us of events and allow us to act on time.

Minimum Test Period: 4 months

Channels: SEO

Set-Up Time	**2**	**Set-Up Cost**	**0**
Recurring Time	**1**	**Recurring Cost**	**2**
Risk	**1**	**ROI**	**2**

43. Grunt Test - Website

Pitch: What if we improved our Grunt Test Score?

Clarification: We could set up a test of our content with carefully selected visitors to get an accurate Grunt Test result.

A grunt test answers the following questions:

1. What do we offer?
2. How does it help our visitors?
3. How should they respond?

The score is based on how long it takes the average visitor to our content to answer the questions above. The standard is under 5 seconds, but faster is better.

Minimum Test Period: 1 month

Channels: Website

Set-Up Time	1	**Set-Up Cost**	0
Recurring Time	0	**Recurring Cost**	0
Risk	1	**ROI**	3

44. Grunt Test – PPC Campaign

Pitch: What if we reviewed all campaigns and graded them on the Grunt Test? Then discontinued the bottom 25% and replaced them with better ideas.

Clarification: In any ecosystem, death is necessary for positive evolution to occur. The only real question is how much death should happen? Campaigns degrade over time, and scheduled reviews can ensure that only our best work is in the market. This process should be conducted twice a year, resulting in 50% freshness annually.

Minimum Test Period: 4 months

Channels: PPC-S, PPC-D

Set-Up Time	2	**Set-Up Cost**	0
Recurring Time	2	**Recurring Cost**	2
Risk	1	**ROI**	2

45. Guest Speaker

Pitch: What if we developed a speaker program and encouraged employees to represent us?

Clarification: Encouraging employees to seek self-improvement in programs like Toastmasters is suitable for everyone. We could create a list of topic areas and survey everyone on their interests in talking about those topics. One side effect of this would be an improvement in the employee's sales presentation skills. Speaking opportunities exist at the local, regional, and national levels.

Minimum Test Period: 12 months

Channels: PR

Set-Up Time	3	**Set-Up Cost**	1
Recurring Time	3	**Recurring Cost**	1
Risk	1	**ROI**	3

46. Guest Blogger

Pitch: What if we identified blogs we would like to be in and pitched tailored articles until they willfully submitted to making us a regular writer?

Clarification: Off-site blogs are SEO gold because they give writers a link that shares their authority to our site. Beyond simply being in the blog, we should have a Google Display Network Campaign drive traffic. This campaign will give the article traffic that will be seen and valued by the blog managers.

Minimum Test Period: 2 months

Channels: SEO, SM,

Set-Up Time	1	**Set-Up Cost**	0
Recurring Time	2	**Recurring Cost**	1
Risk	3	**ROI**	1

47. How-To

Pitch: What if we published a series of How-To articles based on our top 5 products or services?

Clarification: How-to questions about products and services are by far the highest volume of organic searches. Writing articles on How-to use our products or services is a treasure trove of traffic for the Website. Do not forget the most critical How-to subject. How-to pick your business as the supplier. Properly written how-to articles can live a very long time. It is common to find how-to articles contributing traffic years or even decades after it was written.

Minimum Test Period: 4-12 months

Channels: SEO, SM

Set-Up Time	3	**Set-Up Cost**	1
Recurring Time	0	**Recurring Cost**	0
Risk	3	**ROI**	3

48. Intent Only Keywords

Pitch: What if we changed our PPC-S keywords to only those with specific purchase intent?

Clarification: Intent keywords are phrases that show a specific intent to engage or purchase. Examples would be a Personal Injury Lawyer that advertises for "Car Accidents," a topic search. The intent search to this would be "Car Accident Lawyer" or "Car Accident Attorney." The intent extension will lower the quantity but increase quality.

Minimum Test Period: 4-12 months

Channels: PPC-S

Set-Up Time	2	**Set-Up Cost**	2
Recurring Time	0	**Recurring Cost**	0
Risk	1	**ROI**	2

49. Ideal Customer

Pitch: What if we create a model of our ideal customer and build campaigns to target each Ideal-Customer Group?

Clarification: The ideal customer is based on the value we deliver to that group, not just the revenue. Like all campaigns, the tighter the target, the more effective the message delivery can be. In this project, the model should apply to no more than 20% of the customer base. The ideal customer model should be no more than 20% of the market. Ideal Customer Models should include both demographic and firmographic profiles.

Minimum Test Period: 4 Months

Channels: PPC-D, SEO

Set-Up Time	2	**Set-Up Cost**	0
Recurring Time	1	**Recurring Cost**	2
Risk	3	**ROI**	3

50. Invite a Guest Blogger

Pitch: What if we invited leading industry names to be Guest Bloggers on our site?

Clarification: We start with topic research on Amazon and then trace it back to businesses that do not represent a competitive risk. This idea could be combined with the Book recommendation to make this even more powerful. We could become an Amazon Affiliate to create even more revenue. Writers are always looking for ways to promote their books and selected properly we can avoid competitive problems.

Minimum Test Period: 6 Months

Channels: SEO, EM, PPC-D

Set-Up Time	1	**Set-Up Cost**	0
Recurring Time	2	**Recurring Cost**	1
Risk	1	**ROI**	2

51. Influence Factor Split Test

Pitch: What if we created a Display ad set for each of the following influence factors? Reciprocity, Commitment, Consistency, Social Proof, Authority/ Influencer, Liking, Scarcity, Fear of Loss, Greed.

Clarification: We know these are significant factors in an advertising call-to-action. This experiment tests which influence attribute works best with our specific product or service. Knowing this allows us to tune other campaigns. This experiment could have meaningful data in 30 days, but it will be at least four months before the data settles down.

Minimum Test Period: 4 Months

Channels: PPC-S, PPC-D

Set-Up Time	3	**Set-Up Cost**	1
Recurring Time	2	**Recurring Cost**	2
Risk	2	**ROI**	2

52. Listen to Customers

Pitch: What if we subscribed to all our customer's email lists and their primary competitors?

Clarification: We could use this knowledge to enhance our relationships by paying attention to them. We would build out a customer monitor account in Gmail and route all the newsletters into the respective client folder with a subfolder for their competitors. Periodically we review these for opportunities.

Minimum Test Period: 6 Months

Channels: EM

Set-Up Time	**3**	**Set-Up Cost**	**0**
Recurring Time	**1**	**Recurring Cost**	**0**
Risk	**1**	**ROI**	**2**

53. Lead Generator

Pitch: What if we created a lead generator specific to our industry and trade and used that as promotional item?

Clarification: A lead generator is something that a targeted prospect would value enough to get them to act. You are reading a lead generator right now. The key is that the prospect values the lead generator enough to engage with your business. It has to be seen as a fair value exchange for permission to communicate. This can be a white paper or an imprinted item. The key is the perceived value in the prospects mind.

Minimum Test Period: 4 Month

Channels: SEO, EM

Set-Up Time	3	**Set-Up Cost**	3
Recurring Time	1	**Recurring Cost**	1
Risk	3	**ROI**	2

54. Leadership

Pitch: What if we serve in an industry group leadership position?

Clarification: This puts us in a position to hear about industry challenges and events before our competitors. Every industry has groups that represent the voice of the industry. Leadership roles consume time and treasure, but it paints us as industry contributors and provides industry insights. This role gives us meaningful items to talk about in our social media and exposure that you cannot buy. The cost reflected in this includes likely membership and donation costs expected of people in leadership roles.

Minimum Test Period: 1 Year

Channels: SEO, EM

Set-Up Time	2	**Set-Up Cost**	1
Recurring Time	3	**Recurring Cost**	2
Risk	2	**ROI**	3

55. Looking Back

Pitch: What if we looked back five or more years for long-term patterns?

Clarification: The further back you look, the more into the future you can see. Businesses often become myopic when they examine their data. Our thinking becomes focused only on the present, and we fail to see the longer term. This can make us tactically smart and strategically dumb because we do not look back far enough. Industries tend to recycle topics and trends, so looking way back can create the advantage of looking forward.

Minimum Test Period: 1 Year

Channels: All

Set-Up Time	**2**	**Set-Up Cost**	**0**
Recurring Time	**1**	**Recurring Cost**	**0**
Risk	**1**	**ROI**	**2**

56. Listen to Competitors

Pitch: What if we subscribe to every competitor's email list and create market responses to every offer they make in the market?

Clarification: If we listen carefully, we can drive competitors crazy and get them to do something dumb. For example, if a competitor puts an item on sale. We reduce the same item one penny more without putting it on sale.

Minimum Test Period: 4 Months

Channels: EM

Set-Up Time	2	**Set-Up Cost**	0
Recurring Time	2	**Recurring Cost**	0
Risk	1	**ROI**	1

57. Liking

Pitch: What if we created a campaign to improve our likability?

Clarification: People do business with those they like, and they like those that help them understand. Using this basic concept, we create a campaign that educates our market on what we can do for them. Marketing through education is a powerful concept that we can leverage with our blog, email list, and social media.

Minimum Test Period: 4 Months

Channels: SM, EM, Blog

Set-Up Time	**3**	**Set-Up Cost**	**1**
Recurring Time	**3**	**Recurring Cost**	**1**
Risk	**2**	**ROI**	**2**

58. Loosen Keywords

Pitch: What if we loosened keywords and increased PPC volume?

Clarification: Over time, keywords become too tight, and we lose good quality traffic. Negative keywords are rarely reviewed and can be a silent traffic killer.

Minimum Test Period: 4 months

Channels: PPC-S

Set-Up Time	2	**Set-Up Cost**	0
Recurring Time	1	**Recurring Cost**	2
Risk	3	**ROI**	2

59. Marathon

Pitch: What if we ran a Marathon or Ironman Triathlon?

Clarification: This is a PR stunt tied to our social media, blog, and advertising. We could print an event T-Shirt unique to the event to extend the life of the event. Find a Non-Profit you love and make this into a fund-raising event for them.

Minimum Test Period: 4 Months

Channels: SM

Set-Up Time	**1**	**Set-Up Cost**	**2**
Recurring Time	**1**	**Recurring Cost**	**1**
Risk	**3**	**ROI**	**2**

60. Marketing & Sales Team

Pitch: What if we paired up marketing team members with Sales Reps?

Clarification: Marketing staff can become too distant from the customers. Teaming them up with Sales Reps can help them better understand customers and how to communicate with them. This periodic refreshing of the connection to actual customers is critical to the role of marketing. Scheduling should make sure that marketing specialists get exposure to all the ideal customer models.

Minimum Test Period: 1 Month

Channels: SM

Set-Up Time	1	**Set-Up Cost**	2
Recurring Time	1	**Recurring Cost**	1
Risk	1	**ROI**	2

61. Mentoring

Pitch: What if we created a mentoring program for all sales-related positions?

Clarification: Mentors would be responsible for working with the mentee on all significant proposals and meetings. Mentors are not supervisors or managers; they are peers. While a mentor relationship can be reciprocal, that is not common. Mentors need to be trained because the role is not something that everyone has experienced.

Minimum Test Period: 12 Months

Channels: All

Set-Up Time	3	**Set-Up Cost**	1
Recurring Time	3	**Recurring Cost**	3
Risk	3	**ROI**	3

62. Meet new people

Pitch: What if we had every customer-facing person with a goal of meeting new people each week?

Clarification: There is no doubt that a business's contacts and the quality of those contacts are related to success. An organization's voice is a collection of our people's voices, so building the size and quality of those networks is strategic. We know that the simple act of measuring this metric will improve it. There should be no attempt to sell to new contacts. Make these goals public and create awards for top performers.

Minimum Test Period: 12 Months

Channels: SM, EM

Set-Up Time	1	**Set-Up Cost**	1
Recurring Time	2	**Recurring Cost**	1
Risk	1	**ROI**	3

63. Moonshot

Pitch: What if we find a Moonshot innovation, skip risk assessment, and take a chance?

Clarification: Moonshots are big ideas that reinvent your business and your industry. Risk assessment cannot be done because moonshots are always high risk. Moonshots are for mature businesses that have reached the point of reinvention. Do not ask customers about a moonshot idea because they will not understand it. **Trust your judgment and take a risk.** To quote Henry Ford, "*If I had asked my customers what they wanted, I would be raising faster horses*." Don't raise horses when you should be building cars.

Minimum Budget: 20% of marketing budget

Minimum Test Period: 12 months

Channels: All

Set-Up Time	3	**Set-Up Cost**	1
Recurring Time	3	**Recurring Cost**	3
Risk	3	**ROI**	3

64. Map Optimization

Pitch: What if we earned a first position on the Google Map?

Clarification: Maps are driven by reviews making this a project of improving review volume and rating. Reviews are driven by asking for reviews and providing **services worth talking about.**

Minimum Test Period: 6 Months

Channels: SEO

Set-Up Time	1	**Set-Up Cost**	0
Recurring Time	2	**Recurring Cost**	1
Risk	3	**ROI**	3

65. Neighborhood

Pitch: What if we dominated our local neighborhood?

Clarification: We tightly define the local neighborhood and then target that with a Top of Page strategy in PPC and SEO. Many businesses over-reach their geo-target, and this fixes that. This is the classic strategy of a large fish in a small pond. Get to know the target personally, walk the houses, create neighborhood-specific offers, and crush your competitors on your home turf. This strategy reduces operational costs by keeping resources and people closer to the business location.

Minimum Test Period: 4 Months

Channels: PPC-S, PPC-D, SEO

Industries: Home Services, Brick & Mortar Stores

Set-Up Time	2	**Set-Up Cost**	1
Recurring Time	2	**Recurring Cost**	3
Risk	3	**ROI**	2

66. New Product Intro

Pitch: What if we presented a new product to our existing customers?

Clarification: The knee-jerk reaction to this is that we already do this. The challenge is that in marketing, we must repeat ourselves. Have we made sure that customers heard what we told them? This is the old-school concept of talking to customers with one message and making sure it gets delivered. People natively do not like repeating themselves, but frequency of message delivery is the foundation of marketing.

Minimum Test Period: 1 month

Channels: All

Set-Up Time	1	**Set-Up Cost**	0
Recurring Time	2	**Recurring Cost**	2
Risk	2	**ROI**	1

67. New Business Award

Pitch: What if we created a new business award to recognize businesses for Innovation, Management, Public Service, Advocacy, Community, or Technology?

Clarification: Providing leadership for a business award creates many advantages, from asking for nominations to the award event itself. Creating an award is not a low-cost idea and must be widely supported with PPC, SEO, Print, TV, Radio, and other channels.

Minimum Test Period: 6 months

Channels: All

Set-Up Time	3	**Set-Up Cost**	1
Recurring Time	2	**Recurring Cost**	1
Risk	3	**ROI**	2

68. New Value or Industry

Pitch: What if we can find a new use or value for an old product?

Clarification: By exploring sales of old products, can we find a value that we did not expect? Did we sell a product to a customer that we did not expect to buy? Call and find out what their use was. We may find industries and uses that were overlooked that represent new opportunities.

Minimum Test Period: 3 months

Channels: PH, ZM

Set-Up Time	**1**	**Set-Up Cost**	**0**
Recurring Time	**1**	**Recurring Cost**	**1**
Risk	**1**	**ROI**	**3**

69. Non-Profit

Pitch: What if we search for a non-profit synergy and contribute to their mission?

Clarification: Doing good does not exclude doing well, so finding synergy with a non-profit is not only possible it is likely. Promoting the non-profit can promote your business by association. Tracking the performance of these investments is more difficult because they are not commonly designed for tracking.

Minimum Test Period: 6 months

Channels: All

Set-Up Time	2	**Set-Up Cost**	2
Recurring Time	2	**Recurring Cost**	2
Risk	1	**ROI**	2

70. Purple Cow

Pitch: What if we can create a Purple Cow?

Clarification: The term Purple Cow comes from a book by Seth Godin of the same title. A Purple Cow is something worth talking about, worth noticing, exceptional, new, and interesting. It does not have to be high cost, and it could be as simple as using a different color on your product. The key is that it is unexpected and worth talking about. Purple cows cannot be copied or repeated because using it removes its purple, and now it's just a cow.

Minimum Test Period: 6 months

Channels: All

Set-Up Time	1	**Set-Up Cost**	1
Recurring Time	2	**Recurring Cost**	2
Risk	3	**ROI**	3

71. Photo Contest

Pitch: What if we sponsored a Photo Contest for something fun and related to our business?

Clarification: Things like the ugliest dog contest with a relationship to your brand. Contests draw lots of attention for a small amount of money. Part of the contest's value is the winner's bragging rights, which costs nothing. If we can find a contest that can be on-going, that is even better. For example, a local news station has a #BeOnKSBY program that submits pretty nature-themed photos featured on the news. They have run this daily contest for years, and it is still going strong.

Minimum Test Period: 6 months

Channels: Social Media, SEO

Set-Up Time	1	**Set-Up Cost**	1
Recurring Time	1	**Recurring Cost**	2
Risk	3	**ROI**	3

72. Public Event

Pitch: What if we go to a public event dressed up as the animal that best represents our business?

Clarification: I have a friend whose business provides high-speed internet, and his animal of choice is a Cheetah. The connection is that internet connections should be fast, and cheetahs are fast. He goes to events wearing ears and a tail on his business suit, and people love it, and they get the message loud and clear. It is common for keynote speakers to point this out to the crowd!

Minimum Test Period: 12 months

Channels: SM, PPC-D, Live Events

Set-Up Time	**1**	**Set-Up Cost**	**1**
Recurring Time	**1**	**Recurring Cost**	**1**
Risk	**2**	**ROI**	**2**

73. Podcast

Pitch: What if we publish a Podcast on what our prospective customers do?

Clarification: This idea is an extension of the marketing through education idea. Podcasts are interviews, and creating an exciting collection of prospective customers is all we have to do. Find a common theme and interview them on what they are good at. This process will get us time with people and create goodwill we would never normally get.

Minimum Test Period: 12 Months

Channels: PPC-D, SM, EM

Set-Up Time	3	**Set-Up Cost**	1
Recurring Time	3	**Recurring Cost**	3
Risk	3	**ROI**	3

74. Recurring Revenue

Pitch: What if we find a recurring revenue idea for existing customers?

Clarification: Maintenance and repair related to initial sales are often overlooked. As an example, a plumber might install a water heater. This opens the possibility of a water leak monitor service or scheduled water heater maintenance. What have we sold in the past that represents service in the future?

Minimum Test Period: 12 months

Channels: EM, PH

Set-Up Time	**2**	**Set-Up Cost**	**1**
Recurring Time	**1**	**Recurring Cost**	**1**
Risk	**1**	**ROI**	**2**

75. Race to the Bottom

Pitch: What if we reduced PPC bids until we could not spend all the budget?

Clarification: PPC systems are designed to encourage higher bids for higher positions. The logic goes that the higher the position, the more clicks, and the more sales. What if we turn this logic upside down and reduced bids? We would lower the position by reducing the bids, potentially buying more visitors at a lower cost per click. This logic works in campaigns where there is more traffic to buy than budget to buy it with.

Minimum Test Period: 3 Months

Channels: PPC-S, PPC-D

Set-Up Time	1	**Set-Up Cost**	0
Recurring Time	1	**Recurring Cost**	0
Risk	3	**ROI**	3

76. Reciprocity

Pitch: What if we created a campaign to build reciprocity with our prospects or customers?

Clarification: Reciprocity is one of the most potent weapons of influence on our marketing toolbelt. Studies have shown that there is leverage between the value of the gift and the reaction's value. A gift of a $2 item can create a reciprocal action of thousands. This idea is the basis of some of the world's greatest marketing campaigns. Let's put it to work for us.

Minimum Test Period: 6 Months

Channels: SM, EM, PPC-S, PPC-D

Set-Up Time	2	**Set-Up Cost**	2
Recurring Time	2	**Recurring Cost**	2
Risk	3	**ROI**	3

77. Rural or Metro

Pitch: What if we created a campaign targeted at rural areas instead of averaging them in with Metros?

Clarification: Rural areas are often less competitive, allowing reduced marketing costs. Different products or services perform differently in Rural and Metro markets. E-commerce sites often find that rural markets perform better because they do not have as many Brick & Mortar options. The more the consumer is comforted by the Brick & Mortar, the more the Rural performance improves. This performance is primarily driven by the lack of Brick & Mortar stores within the rural communities.

Minimum Test Period: 4 Months

Channels: PPC-S, PPC-D

Set-Up Time	**1**	**Set-Up Cost**	**0**
Recurring Time	**1**	**Recurring Cost**	**1**
Risk	**1**	**ROI**	**3**

78. Silo

Pitch: What if we build out Keyword Silos using existing content?

Clarification: Silos are a well-known SEO strategy and contribute to PPC quality score. Silos are hub pages that bring distributed content together. Many blogs will have hundreds of articles that can be put into a Silo page collection dedicated to a single keyword. Many Content Management Systems like WordPress have indexes built from article tags, but those pages are not optimized for the word. For sites organized by product hierarchy, Benefit Silos can give an effective back door to the content.

Minimum Test Period: 4 Months

Channels: SEO, PPC-S

Set-Up Time	2	**Set-Up Cost**	2
Recurring Time	1	**Recurring Cost**	1
Risk	1	**ROI**	3

79. Social Influencers

Pitch: What if we reached out and connected with social media influencers in our market as a sponsor?

Clarification: Social Influencers is a new word for a celebrity spokesperson. Their value comes from their social media audience. Not all social influencers have massive audiences making them a reasonable strategy for a small business. Big businesses have used celebrity power for generations, but it is a newer tool for small businesses.

Minimum Test Period: 12 month

Channels: SM, SEO

Set-Up Time	2	**Set-Up Cost**	1
Recurring Time	1	**Recurring Cost**	3
Risk	1	**ROI**	3

80. Social Networks

Pitch: What if we worked on increasing our collective social network?

Clarification: Some people within our business have large social networks, but they are not organized and systematically built. This project will identify prospects and process connection requests. While we measure performance by volume of connections, there is a clear quality component in this strategy. Concurrent with building up the network will be a messaging strategy with collateral marketing materials. The connections are the voice, but the materials are what you say.

Minimum Test Period: 12 months

Channels: SM

Set-Up Time	**1**	**Set-Up Cost**	**1**
Recurring Time	**1**	**Recurring Cost**	**1**
Risk	**1**	**ROI**	**1**

81. Social Proof

Pitch: What if we created a campaign to increase our Social Proof?

Clarification: Social Proof is a primary influence factor in our marketing. Social Proof is **"What others say,"** and on the internet, that means reviews. Building reviews requires asking for them and addressing any issues raised. Reviews are not a fine wine; they do not get better with age, and we need a steady stream from a consistent process.

Requesting a review from a customer needs to be as consistent as asking for invoice payment.

Minimum Test Period: 4 Months

Channels: SM

Set-Up Time	**1**	**Set-Up Cost**	**1**
Recurring Time	**1**	**Recurring Cost**	**2**
Risk	**1**	**ROI**	**2**

82. Soundbites

Pitch: What if we identified all our business soundbites and then built a campaign to push these into the market?

Clarification: A soundbite is 9 seconds out of our 20-minute business presentation or the sensational few words that news crews pull out of hours of debate. Identifying that 9 seconds is critical to our core messages. Soundbites are about aligning with the audience's pain and finding the words that move them to action. Identifying these is a feed to many of this book's ideas so extracting them has value beyond this idea.

Minimum Test Period: 6 months

Channels: SM, Blog, PPC-Headlines

Set-Up Time	2	**Set-Up Cost**	1
Recurring Time	1	**Recurring Cost**	2
Risk	2	**ROI**	1

83. Stop Wasting 50%

Pitch: What if we could identify all or part of our wasted budget?

Clarification: The simple discussion of what waste is can go on for days. If it takes 20 touches to move a customer to the desired action, are any of those wasted? How do we know? The question with this one is, do we think we can isolate and measure waste? If we can measure our waste, then we can go after fixing it.

Minimum Test Period: 12 months

Channels: All

Set-Up Time	3	**Set-Up Cost**	0
Recurring Time	2	**Recurring Cost**	1
Risk	2	**ROI**	2

84. Scarcity

Pitch: What if we could create the illusion or reality of scarcity?

Clarification: Scarcity, also known as Fear of Loss, is a primary call to action influencer, and it can be real or perceived. The toy industry has made an art form out of managing scarcity, and it happens to the popular toy of the year. If you think this is an accident, you need to pay closer attention and manage your scarcity.

Minimum Test Period: 3 months

Channels: SM

Set-Up Time	2	**Set-Up Cost**	1
Recurring Time	3	**Recurring Cost**	3
Risk	3	**ROI**	2

85. Single Keyword Ad group

Pitch: What if we took our Top 10 keywords and created a no-compromise sales experience for them?

Clarification: This would include a unique ad and landing page that speaks only to that search. Keyword strategies are a balance between quality and quantity. Anything more than one keyword in an Ad Group and the landing page experience is compromised.

Minimum Test Period:

Channels: PPC-S

Set-Up Time	3	**Set-Up Cost**	0
Recurring Time	1	**Recurring Cost**	3
Risk	1	**ROI**	2

86. Survive

Pitch: What if we found a customer survival attribute in a product or service?

Clarification: Many propose that the primitive concerns of survive or thrive are what drive the market. Is there something about our product or service that goes to customer's survival? If that is the basis of our campaign, it will be wildly successful.

Minimum Test Period:

Channels: PPC-S, PPC-D, SM, SEO

Set-Up Time	3	**Set-Up Cost**	0
Recurring Time	1	**Recurring Cost**	3
Risk	2	**ROI**	2

87. Structured Data

Pitch: What if we optimized the website with a structured data update?

Clarification: Structured data is good SEO because it helps the search engines understand our website content. Websites are written in HTML, a free-format text markup that controls what the browser displays. One weakness of HTML is that it lacks data classification tags making it difficult for search engines to understand the text. For example, how a search engine indexes the word Orange varies by context. In an address or city, it is a formal name, but it could be a fruit, color, or any number of other things in general text. Structured data helps but does not fix this problem. The search engine understands the Orange is a street name with structured data, and it removes it from a recipe search.

Minimum Test Period: 4 Months

Channels: SEO

Set-Up Time	3	**Set-Up Cost**	0
Recurring Time	1	**Recurring Cost**	0
Risk	2	**ROI**	2

88. T-Shirts

Pitch: What if we designed company T-shirts with messaging worth talking about.

Clarification: T-Shirts and other promotional items can put your business in places nothing else will. The key to this is to get a design that people will wear and talk about. Most of the time, this means connecting it to something that the person cares about. Create an excellent T-Shirt design, and you can get large audiences advertising your business and possibly creating a new revenue source.

Minimum Test Period: 6 Months

Channels: SM

Set-Up Time	2	**Set-Up Cost**	2
Recurring Time	1	**Recurring Cost**	2
Risk	1	**ROI**	2

89. TEDx Speaker

Pitch: What if we get invited as a TEDx speaker?

Clarification: TED is a major national brand, and being a TED speaker screams credibility. TEDx is a sub-brand of TED for locally sponsored events. We can set our goal on TED, but it will have to be earned at TEDx first. A TEDx speaking slot is 18 minutes of fame, and the TEDx program is the place to start as a professional speaker.

Minimum Test Period: 2 Years

Channels: SM, SEO

Set-Up Time	3	**Set-Up Cost**	1
Recurring Time	3	**Recurring Cost**	1
Risk	3	**ROI**	3

90. Time on Site

Pitch: What if we could increase our visitor's time-on-site by one minute?

Clarification: Time on Site is a quality of visit metric, and the more time they give you, the more engaged they tend to be. When measuring this, it must be balanced with the quantity of traffic. To get a good measurement, we have to remove the outlier data of very extended stays. One way might be to limit the time-on-site as a maximum multiple of the average. The big push here is creating engaging content and evaluating exit points.

Minimum Test Period: 4 Months

Channels: All

Set-Up Time	2	**Set-Up Cost**	0
Recurring Time	3	**Recurring Cost**	0
Risk	2	**ROI**	1

91. Touchpoints

Pitch: What if we audited all our touch points for brand standards, volumes, measurements, and opportunity?

Clarification: Touchpoints are documents or events that a customer encounters throughout their experience with our business. Documents like invoices, delivery documents, statements, ads, and webpages or events like phone calls, meetings, or emails. The audit is to take a comprehensive view of the experience for consistency to brand and to message. Over time things can go sideways, and a regular audit can reveal issues.

Minimum Test Period: 2 Months

Channels: All

Set-Up Time	2	**Set-Up Cost**	0
Recurring Time	1	**Recurring Cost**	0
Risk	0	**ROI**	1

92. Top 20% Customers

Pitch: What if we audited our Top 20% of Customers to find patterns that we can leverage?

Clarification: 80/20 rules in business are legend. In this project, we identify Top 20% of Customers under two measures, quality, and quantity. Quantity is easy since that is predominantly sales volume. Quality is more difficult to get because it weights the customers who get the maximum value and have the most profound relationship with the business. These are easy for people in the business to identify because these are the customers that the staff loves. If a customer's caller id causes our staff to smile, they are on the quality Top 20.

Minimum Test Period: 3 Months

Channels: All

Set-Up Time	**1**	**Set-Up Cost**	**0**
Recurring Time	**1**	**Recurring Cost**	**1**
Risk	**1**	**ROI**	**2**

93. Tell a Client

Pitch: What if we told customers every time they inspire us?

Clarification: Catching a customer or prospect doing something good and recognizing this can help build relationships. This project would look for ways to monitor good behavior and think deeply about how we say thanks. This has to be authentic and cannot be forced.

Minimum Test Period: 12 Months

Channels: SM, Blog

Set-Up Time	**1**	**Set-Up Cost**	**0**
Recurring Time	**2**	**Recurring Cost**	**1**
Risk	**1**	**ROI**	**2**

94. Split-Test Competition

Pitch: What if we create a split-test competition?

Clarification: Split tests in digital marketing are a best practice, but they can become dull and routine. Track how many times an ad has won a split test and use that as points. Then each cycle, you auction off the ad sets that need a new test. The winner is the person that ends with the most points. Make sure that staff understands that they need to take risks and push boundaries. Accept failures, brush them off, and get back up. The competition should have a reward and bragging rights.

Minimum Test Period: 12 Months

Channels: All

Set-Up Time	2	**Set-Up Cost**	1
Recurring Time	2	**Recurring Cost**	2
Risk	1	**ROI**	3

95. Toastmasters

Pitch: What if we invested in the development of a business spokesperson?

Clarification: Assign a spokesperson and invest in developing their presentation skills. Have them join Toastmasters and win a Regional or higher contest. Focus the talk on the mission of your business or your "Why." Create a reward incentive for winning a regional competition or finding another audience. This is a significant effort, so make sure you include the significate other in the reward. Think about dinner for two at a 5-star restaurant with limo service - do this one right.

Minimum Test Period: 6 Months

Channels: SM, SEO

Set-Up Time	1	**Set-Up Cost**	1
Recurring Time	1	**Recurring Cost**	1
Risk	2	**ROI**	2

96. Trust

Pitch: What if we developed a campaign to build trust with our customers and prospects?

Clarification: Based on this principle:

People do business with those they trust.

They trust those that help them understand.

Start a Marketing-through-education campaign. Help prospects and customers understand the value you create and why they can trust you. Building trust takes a thousand positive outcomes, but only one aw-shucks to reset the counter.

Minimum Test Period: 12 Months

Channels: All

Set-Up Time	**2**	**Set-Up Cost**	**1**
Recurring Time	**1**	**Recurring Cost**	**1**
Risk	**1**	**ROI**	**2**

97. Thrive

Pitch: What if we found ways to help our customers thrive?

Clarification: Ask what we do to help customers thrive? Can we help them reach out? Can we provide social proof of their value? Can we help them build a tribe? Can we provide reviews or high-value backlinks? The success of our customers drives our success, so it makes sense to invest in these areas.

Minimum Test Period: 12 Months

Channels: All

Set-Up Time	2	**Set-Up Cost**	0
Recurring Time	1	**Recurring Cost**	2
Risk	1	**ROI**	2

98. Targeting Competitors

Pitch: What if we went after competitor's brands and trademarks and positioned our business as a logical second opinion or option?

Clarification: Search for competitor brands and trademarks are indications of the vendor selection activity. This traffic is a precious late purchase-cycle search, and some percentage of the audience is open to a second opinion or bid. This idea can be legally dangerous, and Cease-and-Desist letters do happen if you get too bold. In marketing, if you are not offending someone, you are not yet doing your job.

Warning: Talk to your lawyer before investing in this idea.

Minimum Test Period: 4 Months

Channels: PPC-S

Set-Up Time	1	**Set-Up Cost**	1
Recurring Time	2	**Recurring Cost**	3
Risk	3	**ROI**	1

99. Timing is Everything

Pitch: What if we could identify events that trigger movement in the purchase cycle?

Clarification: Everyone agrees that it is better to be lucky than smart. Luck is often more associated with good timing, and some of this can be detected. How can we monitor for events that apply to our business and then act on that event? In the snow removal business, there is nothing better for business than a good snowstorm. What is your snowstorm?

Minimum Test Period: 6 Months

Channels: PPC-S

Set-Up Time	3	**Set-Up Cost**	1
Recurring Time	3	**Recurring Cost**	2
Risk	1	**ROI**	3

100. Tighten Keywords

Pitch: What if we tightened keywords with better matching and negatives?

Clarification: Keywords start very broad, and as data builds, there is an opportunity to tighten them up and get better performance from the PPC investment. Data makes us more intelligent, but we still have to act on that knowledge. If the budget is constrained, meaning that there is more traffic to buy than money to buy it with. Then tightening keywords can be an opportunity.

Minimum Test Period: 4 Months

Channels: PPC-S

Set-Up Time	3	**Set-Up Cost**	0
Recurring Time	3	**Recurring Cost**	2
Risk	3	**ROI**	2

101. Translation

Pitch: What if we translated our website content to another language?

Clarification: Expanding our content into another language can open new markets to our business. The content we already have can be translated leveraging the content creation investment. Translating content is never 100% leverage, but the base content can often be 80% of the time and effort.

Minimum Test Period: 12 Months

Channels: All

Set-Up Time	3	**Set-Up Cost**	2
Recurring Time	1	**Recurring Cost**	1
Risk	1	**ROI**	2

102. Viral Video

Did you notice? We could not help ourselves? The cover promises 100 ideas, but the book delivers 106. We always strive to deliver more than we promise.

Pitch: What if we could create a viral video related to our industry?

Clarification: Creating a viral video is the holy grail of digital marketing. Nobody has found the secret formula, but who is to say that it will not be us? We know a few things about viral and one is that you cannot copy from someone else's success. The surprise of the content is what makes it worth being viral. From the Dancing Baby in 1996 to The Dress in 2015, viral content is the stuff of legends in marketing. Going viral is a high-risk, high-reward strategy, but please step up and tell the story if you have the right stuff.

Minimum Test Period: 2 Months

Channels: SM, SEO

Set-Up Time	3	**Set-Up Cost**	1
Recurring Time	0	**Recurring Cost**	0
Risk	3	**ROI**	3

103. Webinar

Pitch: What if we could create a webinar to share our expertise with our customers and prospects?

Clarification: Creating a webinar is a part of the marketing through education strategy. Find the most common questions from customers and prospects and then answer them with a 20-minute live presentation. Then promote the live event. The entire event is 45 minutes, with the remaining time filled with questions and answers.

Minimum Test Period: 4 Months

Channels: TC, SM, SEO

Set-Up Time	3	**Set-Up Cost**	1
Recurring Time	2	**Recurring Cost**	2
Risk	1	**ROI**	3

104. Whale Campaign

Pitch: What if we could bring in a Whale account?

Clarification: In marketing terms, a Whale is a huge account, and many small businesses assume they cannot get that business. While marketing to these is different, it is not impossible. If you never ask Whales for their business, you will never get it. Failing to act causes 100% failure guaranteed. Whales are the kind of account that makes sales superheroes. Call on the big guys because sometimes they say yes. Don't bet-the-farm on a whale account but also do not ignore the opportunity.

Minimum Test Period: 12 Months

Channels: PH, EM

Set-Up Time	1	**Set-Up Cost**	1
Recurring Time	2	**Recurring Cost**	2
Risk	3	**ROI**	3

105. Why-to

Pitch: What if we wrote a series of Why-to articles?

Clarification: Why-to is a high-volume search typically positioned in the early stages of a purchase cycle. Properly written Why-to articles can live a very long time. It is common to find why-to articles contributing traffic to the website years or even decades after it was written.

Minimum Test Period: 12 Months

Channels: SEO, PPC-S, PPC-D

Set-Up Time	**3**	**Set-Up Cost**	**1**
Recurring Time	**0**	**Recurring Cost**	**0**
Risk	**1**	**ROI**	**3**

106. Write a Book

Pitch: What if we wrote a book about our superpowers and distributed them to our customers and prospects?

Clarification: Nothing puts a stake in the ground about your business value to your customer, like writing a book to share your value and expertise. Get the book released in print and e-book formats in Amazon and IngramSpark. Get extra points for a best seller rating!

Minimum Test Period: 12 Months

Channels: PPC-D, SEO, Social Media

Set-Up Time	3	**Set-Up Cost**	2
Recurring Time	0	**Recurring Cost**	1
Risk	3	**ROI**	2

107. Zoom

Pitch: What if we could move more customer communications to Zoom from the Phone or Email?

Clarification: Zoom, Microsoft Teams, Webex, GoToMeeting, and all the other video conferencing software is a step up in communication quality when used correctly. Did you notice that comma? Used properly requires that business train their team on how to present in the video. Issues like Attire, Voice, Manners, and others have been overlooked by many. This project is about doing this right. Anyone can install and run the software, but do you want your business to be the next viral Lawyer-Kitten (Feb 2021). This was a viral video of a lawyer in a Zoom courtroom that could not turn the kitten filter off. Avoid the Cat-astrophe and give your team professional skills and marketing collateral.

Minimum Test Period: 4 Months

Channels: TC

Set-Up Time	2	**Set-Up Cost**	1
Recurring Time	1	**Recurring Cost**	1
Risk	1	**ROI**	2

Index

SMS
2021
2020

Made in the USA
Monee, IL
04 November 2026

67386436R00075